My Poems

### The Way

What's to do, vicariously ? the way or the end.
may be, ends meet, once in a lifetime!
But, nonetheless, the way is first, say it viciously;
the end next
- nothing less.

The wondrous world starts at the end;
and the way leads.
the evolution is right in the erudite classroom;
but, creationism is also right, in verse.
What comes first chicken or egg?
No one knows for sure !
The way or the end?

What's right for the emperor?
What's wrong? -- turbulence in the air!
I know that you don't, if not like that!

What's to do, vicariously, once again ? the way or the end.
may be, ends meet!
But, nonetheless, the way is first, say it viciously;
the end next
- nothing less.

## The way of a piercing

What's to do, vicariously ? the way or the end.
may be, ends meet, once in a lifetime!
But, nonetheless, the way is first, say it viciously;
the end next
- nothing less.

The wondrous world starts at the end;
and the way leads.
the evolution is right in the erudite classroom;
but, creationism is also right, in verse.
What comes first chicken or egg?
No one knows for sure !
The way or the end?

What's right for the emperor?
What's wrong? -- turbulence in the air!
I know that you don't, if not like that!

What's to do, vicariously, once again ? the way or the end.
may be, ends meet!
But, nonetheless, the way is first, say it viciously;
the end next
- nothing less.

### The way is a device

What's to do, vicariously ? the way or the end.
may be, ends meet, once in a lifetime!
But, nonetheless, the way is first, say it viciously;
the end next
- nothing less.

The wondrous world starts at the end;
and the way leads.
the evolution is right in the erudite classroom;
but, creationism is also right, in verse.
What comes first chicken or egg?
No one knows for sure !
The way or the end?

What's right for the emperor?
What's wrong? -- turbulence in the air!
I know that you don't, if not like that!

What's to do, vicariously, once again ? the way or the end.
may be, ends meet!
But, nonetheless, the way is first, say it viciously;
the end next
- nothing less.

## The way or the end

What's to do in life ? the way or the end
may be ends meet once in a lifetime
But, nonetheless, the way is first, say it
the end next nothing less.

The wondrous world starts at the end, and spirtual healing
and the way leads
the evolution is right in the classroom
but creationism is also right in verse
What comes first chicken or egg
No one knows for sure
The way or the end

What's right for the emperor
What's wrong
I know that you don't, if not like that

What's to do, once again ? the way or the end
may be, ends meet
But nonetheless the way is first, say it loud
the end next nothing less.

## A way of life

What's to do in life ? A way or the end
may be ends meet once in a lifetime
But, nonetheless, the way is first, say it
the end next nothing less.

## The well is near the way

What's to do in life ? the way or the end
may be ends meet once in a lifetime
But, nonetheless, the way is first, say it
the end next nothing less.

The wondrous world starts at the end
and the way leads
the evolution is right in the classroom
but creationism is also right in verse
What comes first chicken or egg
No one knows for sure
The way or the end

What's right for the emperor
What's wrong
I know that you don't, if not like that

What's to do, once again ? the way or the end
may be, ends meet
But nonetheless the way is first, say it loud
the end next nothing less.

## The memoir of way of life

What's to do in life ? the way or the end
may be ends meet once in a lifetime
But, nonetheless, the way is first, say it
the end next nothing less.

The wondrous world starts at the end
and the way leads
the evolution is right in the classroom
but creationism is also right in verse
What comes first chicken or egg
No one knows for sure
The way or the end

What's right for the emperor
What's wrong
I know that you don't, if not like that

What's to do, once again ? the way or the end
may be, ends meet
But nonetheless the way is first, say it loud
the end next nothing less.

### The life of way

What's to do in life ? the way or the end
may be ends meet once in a lifetime
But, nonetheless, the way is first, say it
the end next nothing less.

The wondrous world starts at the end, and spirtual healing
and the way leads
the evolution is right in the classroom
but creationism is also right in verse
What comes first chicken or egg
No one knows for sure
The way or the end
What's right for the emperor

What's wrong
I know that you don't, if not like that

What's to do, once again ? the way or the end
may be, ends meet
But nonetheless the way is first, say it loud
the end next nothing less.

### The way of life
What's to do ? the way or the end
may be ends meet once in a lifetime
But, nonetheless, the way is first, say it
the end next nothing less.

The wondrous world starts at the end
and the way leads
the evolution is right in the classroom
but creationism is also right in verse
What comes first chicken or egg
No one knows for sure
The way or the end

What's right for the emperor
What's wrong
I know that you don't, if not like that

What's to do, once again ? the way or the end
may be, ends meet
But nonetheless the way is first, say it loud
the end next nothing less.

### The way

What's to do ? the way or the end
may be ends meet once in a lifetime
But, nonetheless, the way is first, say it
the end next nothing less.

The wondrous world starts at the end
and the way leads
the evolution is right in the classroom
but creationism is also right in verse
What comes first chicken or egg
No one knows for sure
The way or the end

What's right for the emperor
What's wrong
I know that you don't, if not like that

What's to do,  once again ? the way or the end
may be, ends meet
But nonetheless the way is first, say it loud
the end next nothing less.

## The Way

What's to do, vicariously ? the way or the end.
may be, ends meet, once in a lifetime!
But, nonetheless, the way is first, say it viciously;
the end next
- nothing less.

The wondrous world starts at the end;
and the way leads.
the evolution is right in the erudite classroom;
but, creationism is also right, in verse.
What comes first chicken or egg?
No one knows for sure !
The way or the end?

What's right for the emperor?
What's wrong? -- turbulence in the air!
I know that you don't, if not like that!

What's to do, vicariously, once again ? the way or the end.
may be, ends meet!
But, nonetheless, the way is first, say it viciously;
the end next
- nothing less.

### The way

What's to do, vicariously ? the way or the end.
may be, ends meet, once in a lifetime!
But, nonetheless, the way is first, say it viciously;
the end next
- nothing less.

The wondrous world starts at the end;
and the way leads.
the evolution is right in the erudite classroom;
but, creationism is also right, in verse.
What comes first chicken or egg?
No one knows for sure !
The way or the end?

What's right for the emperor?
What's wrong? -- turbulence in the air!
I know that you don't, if not like that!

What's to do, vicariously,once again ? the way or the end.
may be, ends meet!
But, nonetheless, the way is first, say it viciously;
the end next
- nothing less.

## The vigilant man, I am

I am the vigilant man.
I am the virtuoso.
My wife, she, I see in dire need of me.
My prodigal sons will return some day, if not all like that .
I am the emperor, the wise, the unorthodox, the orthodox.
I am a man, that's all.
The world taxes me along the lines.
Now I am the titan of things.

## My atriculate poem that possibly can ryhme
by Suresh Devanathan

Well, atriculate is a word,
may be, a word for the wise.
wisedom seeks knowledge
I still cannot ryhme, however
I am atriculate, better than to scapgoat my problems, without question
i will ryhme. What a wonderous world, is matriculate the new atriculate
can poems really ryhme?
I told you i will ryhme, may be another time, total spendor of word of the wise, in essense
can it still be the truth??
I told you i will ryhme, may be another time, total spendor of word of the wise, in essense
can it still be the truth?

## The ignormus Neighbor
by Suresh Devanathan

Where in the world are you
You thy Neighbor.
Where would be you, other than near my house
you little girl , my ignormus neighbor
make up and shampoo all over you
the dna

## The Math

## Turing Test Passed!

Suppose i write turing test passed with 100% probability, can you dispute it? if you dispute it, i will simply call you crazy or drawf or idiot! If you say you are harvard, i will say fabricated data! If you come close, i will say non-local is better than local? If you say star, i say star is far, like no wife nor food! So on, and so forth! Then i say alan turing is gay! May be, if the author of the turing test is gay, the assumptions of the test are wrong and turing test passable with 100% probability!

## P=NP

Suppose you have an random number generator. Take the problem of boolean satisfiability. According to Cook's thesis, even if one problem in NP domain provable to P, all of them will be. Take combinational testability. Take a fault and suppose the probability of detecting the fault is p. Now probability of detecting the fault after N interation s if $1-(1-p)^N$ where N is the number of cycles. Suppose you have a finite but large constant K, $\lim_{K \to \infty} 1-(1-p)^K = 1$. The fault detected with 100% probability. Now, to provable that untestability. Suppose p is the probability of detecting the fault, suppose you conduct an experiment and take K random sample to calculate p, the standard deviation is $1/\sqrt{K} \cdot \sigma$, but sigma is at best 1. For finite but large K, $\lim_{K \to \infty}$, suppose the fault is untestable, then p will converge to 0, $1/\sqrt{K}$ is 0.

Proof complete. P=NP and all problems solvable in O(1) time.


For finite cases, with a few exceptions.
I say to err is human. There is no perfect way for the computer or computer programmer to build a perfect program or result verifier with 100% confidence. I say the problem statement is irrelavent.

## Proof of Factorization doable in P time

take the first log(N) primes

now that the probability that the number is factorable by the first
K primes = 1- (1-1/2)*(1-1/3)*(1-1/4)*(1-1/5).... = 1 - 0.56/ log(K)
Now replace K with log(N)

probability = 1 - 0.56/ log(log(N))

As N->infinity
 = 1 - 0.56/infinity
proability = 1

To find the first log(N) it would take log(N)*log(log(N))^3 caculations, since
the test of primality takes log(log(N))^3 calculations

so, factorization is log(N)*log(log(N))^3

## Goldbach Conjecture Proof

let e be the even number
lhs = e + A
rhs = 2+2+A
lim A->infinity    lhs = infinity = rhs = infinity
if lhs = rhs, A's cancel
e = 2+2

every even number is expressible as a sum of two primes

Disproof
let e be the even number
lhs = e + A
rhs = 2+4+A
lim A->infinity    lhs = infinity = rhs = infinity
if lhs = rhs, A's cancel
e = 2+4

## P!=NP Proof

Since the universe is quantum mechanical, probabilistic, there is a possibility that given infinite time and space, a mathematician running computers can observe p!=np. I cite that mathematician.

**Physics**

## Bell Inequality

A random number generator stuck at 1 is experimentally random.
A random number generator stuck at 0 is experimentally random.
A random number generator stuck in the following sequence is still experimentally random

Take CHSH inequality.

A(B+B') + A'(B-B') <= 2

Suppose the random number generator is stuck on the following sequence
let A = 1, B' = 1, B=1 and A'=1

lhs = 1(1+1) + 1(1-1)
    = 2

Now the calculator wont work on finite precision machine

Take a variable x = sqrt(sqrt( ....sqrt(pi).. 50 times)
take y= ((x^2)^2.....)^2 50 times

let z = (y - pi)/(1-pi) = (1-pi)/(1-pi)=1

but z must be 0, but it is 1

lhs = 2 + 0
    = 2+ z
    = 2 + 1   (z=1)
    = 3
3 <=(not) 2

Violates bell inequality.


Bell inequality non violatable

suppose you have  lhs = A(B+B') + A'(B-B')  = 2 + K
  now take
    = 2 + K + 0
    = 2 + K - 0*(K+1)
    = 2 + K - z*(K+1)

= 2 + K - K - 1 (z=1)
= 1